Buying Your First Home?

Insider Secrets You Must Know

I0473886

Chuck Cosmato

Donna Cosmato

DEDICATION

Solio Deo Gloria (Glory to God Alone)

Chuck Cosmato: I dedicate this book to my wife and family as well as all my colleagues and clients.

Donna Cosmato: I dedicate this to my beloved father-in-law (Dad). It's been an honor to work with him in creating this guide for homebuyers. It is also dedicated to my precious mother, who faithfully read each word and found every typo and grammatical error (even the one in this dedication) and to my family.

CONTENTS

ACKNOWLEDGMENTS

Patty Cosmato – Authors' photo, back cover
Michele McDonough – Cover design and graphics
Kate Schubert - Editor

1- ARE YOU PREPARED TO BUY A HOME?

There are many topics discussed in this book such as interviewing real estate agents, viewing homes, making purchase offers, or applying for a mortgage to mention just a few. There is no doubt an entire book could be written about any one of these subjects, but that is not our purpose here.

We want to simplify these large topics into a concise guide that can be read and put to use in the shortest possible time. We hope you enjoy the trip on which you are about to embark, which is the journey to your new home.

Before you hop in the car with your real estate agent or head out on your own to look at homes for sale, do your financial homework. After all, there is no sense in wasting your time and energy looking at houses that are out of your price range.

Weigh the advantages and disadvantages of owning versus renting to see which is most beneficial for your current situation. Consider carefully how much mortgage you can afford so you do not burden yourself with a financial obligation you cannot handle. Once you have done what we like to call your "due diligence," you are better prepared to start house hunting!

What steps do you need to take to find out how much you can afford to spend on your new home? Is it enough to know your income and outgo, or are there more pieces to the puzzle of determining your net worth? You'll discover the answers to these questions as well as many others as you read the following chapters.

We'll launch you on your home buying journey by discussing how you can figure out how much home you can afford, and we will hold your hand while we work through the process together. Let's get started by discovering how much you can afford to spend on your home purchase.

Once you know how much you can afford, you'll have a better idea of where you may have to compromise on the features you want in your new home.

Use the following guide to do your calculations and discover your true net worth. When you know this information, you can make an informed choice about how much you should spend on your housing expenses. You will also learn how to improve your creditworthiness if necessary.

How Do Lenders Make Decisions?

Potential lenders weigh risk versus reward when they evaluate a person's creditworthiness for a loan. They want to know how much you make and from what source(s).

Your credit and employment history must be disclosed to them, and they may ask questions that make you feel uncomfortable or seem intrusive.

If you collect income from a previous spouse or receive child support payments, you will have to disclose that information although they may or may not consider the income when evaluating your application. Your willingness to cooperate with all their requests and provide as much information as you can helps them make their decision.

How Lenders Use the Information You Provide

You furnish data about what type of credit you currently have, how much debt you are carrying, and how much new debt you have recently incurred. How you pay your bills each month and whether you are in arrears affects their final decision.

Once they have gathered all the information about your income and your debt, they do a calculation to determine your debt to income ratio. In other words, they need to know how much discretionary income you have each month after you have paid all your obligations. Traditionally, a debt to income ratio of 36 percent of your gross monthly income is considered to be in the safe zone for individuals wanting to qualify for a loan.

Avoid This Financial Trap

However, there is a danger in this for potential homebuyers. The traditional model is based on calculating a ratio predicated on one's monthly **gross income** rather than **net income**.

If you anticipate any changes in your employment or life such as a layoff or the birth of a new child, it may be wiser to do your calculations based on net income so you have a buffer of protection in case of loss or decline in your income.

Calculating Debt to Income Ratios

You can do your own calculations before you meet with a loan officer to get a better idea of where you stand financially and how much mortgage you can afford.

Use this formula to do your math:

- Gross monthly income (GMI) x 28% = the highest amount you can afford for housing (PITI or principal, interest, taxes and insurance or rent)
- GMI x 36% = the highest amount of overall monthly debt you should carry to afford your mortgage or rent payment

Let's look at an example:

Gross yearly income of $57,000 ($57,000 ÷ 12 = $4750)

GMI = $4750

$4750 x 28% = $1330 maximum PITI or rent

GMI = $4750

$4750 x 36% = $1710 maximum monthly indebtedness

Do you want to do an honest evaluation of your ability to repay a mortgage and discover how much house you can afford? Make a budget worksheet.

Document all your monthly expenditures (no matter how small) and be brutally honest. After all, you are not fooling anyone but yourself. If you get in over your head and cannot afford your mortgage payment, you could end up losing your home or having to file bankruptcy.

What's Your Monthly Expense Situation?

Let's walk through an example to figure this out. While the following is not an inclusive list of the areas you should examine, it is a good starting point for your research.

List your monthly expenditures for items such as:

- Food
- Clothing
- Entertainment
- Transportation
- Vehicle maintenance and fuel
- Health insurance
- Dental, vision and other insurance
- Professional fees and dues
- Childcare
- Credit card debt
- Ongoing education or student loans
- Utilities and amenities such as high speed Internet access or streaming video services
- Miscellaneous expenses such as fitness center memberships or martial arts classes

For the purposes of our exercise, let's assume your total monthly expenses equal **$1052.**

For the next step, total all the income you receive each month from any sources. For this exercise, we want to determine net monthly income (after all taxes and deductions) rather than gross monthly income.

Finally, total up your net monthly income (NMI) and your total monthly expenditures (TME). Subtract the amount of the expenses from your net income. The resulting amount is your disposable monthly income, which you can multiply by 28 percent to determine how much your principal, interest, taxes, and insurance (PITI) should be to give you a hedge of protection.

Example:

$57,000 Gross yearly salary = $45,600 adjusted net yearly income (we are assuming a 20% percent tax/deduction). Our adjusted monthly net equals $3800 ($45,600 ÷ 12).

- NMI = $3800
- TME = $1052
- $3800 - $1052 = $2748
- $2748 x 28% = $769.44

As you can see, by using the net income versus the gross income, we are being more cautious (and realistic) regarding how much mortgage we can afford comfortably.

We can look in a more appropriate price range and avoid over-extending ourselves in housing that is too expensive.

In the current market with an interest rate of about 4 percent, you could borrow about 150,000 on a 30-year fixed mortgage. However, if you could put $50,000 down, you could buy a $200,000 home.

How Can I Improve My Chances of Loan Approval?

What can you do to reduce your monthly expenses so you can afford a more expensive home if that is your desire? Consider paying off your debt; in particular, pay off high interest rate loans and credit cards.

While you could increase your income by working more hours or taking a second job, you have to balance that option with the consequences of such an action.

How will that affect your personal or professional life? Do you really want to work two (or more) jobs for 15 or 30 years just to afford a mortgage payment?

If you really have your heart set on a high priced home, you may have to delay your purchase until you pay down your debt. Other ways to cut your debt load are to reduce or eliminate optional expenses such as cable, landline telephones, or dining out. Lastly, you can save more.

By making a larger down payment, you lower your monthly payment and save on interest charges over the life of the loan.

The good news is because you took the time to assess your financial situation, you are in a better position to make an informed decision about how much you want to pay for your new home and you can answer the question "How much home can I afford?" with confidence.

2 – BUY OR RENT?

Should you buy a home now or rent? While you are probably familiar with the most common reasons for buying versus renting such as acquiring a hard asset, getting tax breaks, or building equity, there are more fulfilling reasons to buy a home.

You'll take control of your housing expenses by establishing a fixed monthly cost, but there are emotional and spiritual reasons that go much deeper than the cold, hard financial facts. Here are four unusual advantages of buying your own home you may not have considered.

You Want to Release Your Inner Artist

Owning your own home gives you the freedom (in most cases) to be as creative as you choose with exterior and interior paint and decorative touches. Before you make a purchase offer on any home, however, it's important to check for any onerous rules that would limit your free use and enjoyment of your residence.

For example, if you purchase a condominium or co-op, which are sometimes referred to as shared-lifestyle homes or common interest developments (CIDs), the use of your property is governed by restrictive covenants called Covenants, Declarations of Conditions, and Restrictions or CC&Rs.

These guidelines dictate where you can park, how many vehicles you can park, and whether or not your guests can park on or off the premises as well as other important lifestyle restrictions. If you are permitted to paint your home's exterior, you must adhere to the CC&R's for your community. On the other hand, it could also mean you are stuck with whatever the exterior color of the house might be.

Does this sounds too confining for your tastes? If you think you can avoid the issue by buying a single-family dwelling, better think again. Many developments and communities have a homeowner's association (HOA) with an accompanying list of rules, regulations and restrictions.

Our point here? If it is important to you to change the exterior color of the house, or if you want to put green shag carpeting in the dining room and burgundy shag carpet in the bedrooms, be extremely meticulous when you create your dream house list and look at properties with your agent.

However, the bottom line is when you own your home, you can change the window treatments, add an extra room onto the house, turn the garage into an apartment or workshop, or enjoy it just the way you bought it. The choices are yours, and this is just one of the advantages of buying your own home rather than renting.

You Love Pets

If you are wondering if you should buy a home now or rent, here's some more food for thought. Whether you already have a pet or pets or you long to add one to your family, the harsh reality is pets and property owners are like oil and water - they just do not mix. Being a pet lover is another one of those excellent reasons to buy a home rather than rent one.

Most landlords are not willing to allow a pet (or pets) on the premises. If they permit you to have a pet, it is almost a given there will be rules and regulations to observe. For instance, they may restrict the height, weight or type of pet.

While dogs and cats are common choices as pets, and some property owners will allow them, what happens if you want to own a bird, a snake, or even a pot-bellied pig? If you think getting a potential property owner to allow you to own a Siamese cat or a Chihuahua is difficult, just image the reaction if you want to include a tarantula, a sugar glider or an exotic pet in your family!

Now, we do not want to sound like we are picking on the landlords of the world because there are some perfectly valid reasons why a property owner would rather not have animals in residence.

Here are just a few:

1. He or she is at risk in cases of loss, injury or damage caused by the animal and could be sued.
2. Removing animal dander and hair from a vacated apartment or a home can be expensive, but it must be done. The next tenant could have an allergic reaction to those allergens.
3. The residence could become infested with pests like fleas or ticks.
4. Even the best-trained, housebroken pet can have an accident, and urine, stains and odors can be difficult to remove from carpets and floors.

The point being, if owning a pet is important to your lifestyle, you are much better off purchasing your own home where you set the rules instead of being subject to someone else's rules.

Case Study

We are intimately acquainted with a family we will call the Anthonys who found themselves in this situation when they married and blended their fur families. Four cats plus two dogs equals trouble if you are considering renting a residence.

Fortunately, they found the perfect solution with their ownership of a quaint ranch style home located on approximately three acres in rural Virginia with a panoramic view of the mountains.

Of course, the new hubby was assigned the task of creating an outdoor enclosure to allow the Chihuahuas some freedom to roam without being snatched up by hawks and eagles. Because they own their home instead of renting, erecting a fenced-in enclosure (complete with metal flashings to contain cats capable of scaling a six-foot fence) was no problem.

Adding Other Pets

As a plus, when a giant mixed breed dog decided to adopt the couple as his very own fur parents, they had plenty of space for him to run, play and exercise. Just imagine trying to tell a property owner you've just adopted a St. Bernard mixed breed dog. We'll leave the response to your imagination, but you might expect it to be negative.

However, we think you get our drift because when you rent, most property owners are hesitant about the whole issue of owning pets. However, they might allow one pet, and you will probably have to pay a sizable damage deposit.

Successful Conclusion

As a final note to this everyone-lived-happily-ever-after story, because the Anthonys own their own home and a significant amount of property, they were able to purchase a large travel trailer and install it on the knoll for the new wife's mom to use as a vacation home when she came to visit them every year.

Hubby created a one-eighth mile walking track that curves around the property so everyone can enjoy the fresh air while they exercise. In addition, their nine-year old son revs up his gasoline-powered go-kart and zooms around the track without causing any complaints.

They plant a small garden each year and enjoy fresh fruits and vegetables during the growing season. We could go on and on but the point is clear. Owning your own home gives you freedom and options you do not have when you rent.

Renters are subject to the landlord's rules and regulations, while in most cases, homeowners set their own regulations and rules. (We'll talk about this more later.)

You Need a Place to Exercise Your Green Thumb

Some individuals satisfy their green thumbs with container or windowsill gardens, but there are those who long for a little patch of earth to transform into a garden.

While most property owners of our acquaintance have no problem with a tenant keeping a well-maintained garden, the issue of size does come into play. If you want to grow more than a few tomatoes or other vegetables, you probably need an area about 10 to 20 feet for a garden patch.

When you are a homeowner, you can opt for a traditional garden or you can utilize an idea from Victorian days and go with a cottage garden, where you fit your plants into little nooks and crannies around the house and landscape.

If you want to add amenities to your garden such as a water fountain or pond, there's nobody to stop you. You can have garden statuary, bird baths, or even waterfalls and rock walls. The only limit to your creativity when you are a homeowner is any CC&Rs or Home Owner Association (HOA) restrictions.

In addition to planting a garden, perhaps you've always longed to do some beautiful landscaping around your property. If you want to plant a living fence of bamboo or other ornamental bushes or shrubs, go right ahead. Your windbreak of Leyland cypress trees may turn out to be a wonderful privacy fence some day.

Love apples but hate the hybrid, genetically modified varieties you find at your local store? Plant your own fruit trees and enjoy your harvest or build a tree house in that stately oak tree that provides you with shade in the spring and summer and glorious foliage in the fall. Remember—**you** are in charge—because you own the property.

You Value Your Privacy

It's been our professional experience that most property owners respect a tenant's rights for privacy. However, it's also true that a landlord does have the right to enter your property. Depending on the laws governing your geographic location, he or she could enter your home at any time and without any prior notice.

The home or apartment you rent may have an excellent security system, but it may not. How would you feel if you wanted to add an extra layer of security with deadbolts or rekeyed locks, but your property owner would not permit it? How about if you wanted to install a security system? These are some of the questions to consider as you are mulling the decision of renting versus buying.

A common thread you probably noticed during our discussion of these four unique advantages of buying your own home is they all revolve around your **freedom**.

If you make a choice to buy in a community with restrictions and regulations, you are still free to exercise your freedom and individuality within the framework of those guidelines. If you choose to purchase a home without any restrictions, you have more freedom and more choices.

However, if you opt for renting, you make yourself subject to the property owner's rules and regulations. Choices have consequences, but not all consequences are negative.

What's your take on this? Is the time right for you to move ahead with a home purchase or should you continue to rent?

3 - YOUR DREAM HOUSE WISH LIST

While we cannot sit down at the kitchen table with you and help you brainstorm ideas for your list, we can give you inspiration on areas to consider and issues to ponder.

Grab a notebook, a pencil or pen, and a cup or glass of your favorite beverage and get ready to do some soul-searching. By investing a little time upfront to think about where you want to live and what you like to do, you avoid making an expensive mistake or finding yourself trapped in a home you hate. In addition, you discover what you really, really want in a home.

Setting aside the basic need for a shelter to protect you from the weather, are you motivated by finances (buying a home may be cheaper than renting) or lifestyle (are you planning to expand your family, or do you need to take care of an aging relative?)

In this chapter, we assume you have gone through the exercise of determining what your budget will be and how much home you can afford, but if not, you can refer back to Chapter 1 for detailed instructions.

In the following sections, there are lots of questions to stimulate your thought process about where you want to live, why you want to own a home, when you want to move into your new residence, and much more. We will help you think through the priorities of your life and define the search criteria for your dream home.

While we cannot promise to discover the perfect home for you, by prodding your intellectual processes and helping you come up with valid requirements to narrow your selection, we will move you closer to that home for which you are longing.

The purpose of going through this questioning process is to help you focus on why you want to own a house, what it would probably look like, how it would fit into your lifestyle, and if it will fulfill your needs such as pride of ownership, independence and convenience. We suggest you write your answers down in a notebook or create a worksheet for your answers.

By necessity, these questions are open-ended and generic to inspire you to think of even more questions about your specific situation and desires. If we could meet with you personally, and we wish we could, we would tailor the questions to your lifestyle, career and preferences.

It will take you some time to work through this list, but it will be worth it. If you don't have the time to devote to it right now, you can always start the process, save your responses, and come back and answer more questions and add more data to your notebook or worksheet as time allows. Just finish your discovery process as it suits your schedule.

Now, let's answer the **who, what, where, when, why** and **how** questions that are the foundation for creating your dream house list.

When Do You Want to Move?

Are you planning to move in the next three months or is home ownership a long-term goal for you? Answering this question first helps you in many ways because if you are hoping to make an immediate move, you'll want to work through the rest of our questions quickly so you can get to the fun part, which is creating your dream house wish list.

If, on the other hand, owning your own home is a dream on your future achievements list, you may want to stop right here for now. After all, if your dream home is five or six years into the future, your lifestyle, occupation and family situation could change dramatically. However, if you have made up your mind that owning a home is the best move for you, then let's get started on figuring out exactly what you want and need.

Who Are You?

Ask yourself these questions to discover not only who you are today but also who you might be in the future:

1. What is your status? Are you single, engaged, divorced, retired, elderly or disabled?
2. Who else will be living with you? How might your situation change in the future?
3. If you are single, do you plan to live alone or will you find a roommate?
4. What will you do if you have to add someone to your household unexpectedly such as an aging relative, a foster child, a sibling, or even a pet?

As you worked through this list, you probably thought of other questions or concerns you might have about how your new home will affect your lifestyle. Jot down the answers to those as well, so you can include those thoughts in your finished wish list.

Who's Going to Live There and Why?

Knowing who will live in the house, listing the reasons why they will be living there, and understanding the requirements of their lifestyles is a big help in setting the search parameters for your new home.

Think about these questions as you develop your wish list:

1. Are you expecting children either now or in the immediate future?
2. Are you planning to have any children at all?
3. How many pets (if any) do you own?
4. Are you planning to acquire any pets in the future?
5. What sizes and types of pets might you decide to own and how much yard space would be required?
6. Will you have the responsibility of caring for an elderly relative or close friend?

7. Will this mean you need to opt for a ranch style home with no stairs or a home that can be remodeled for accessibility?
8. Where will you be in your career in the next five to ten years?
9. How will that affect your lifestyle and your housing requirements?
10. How much time will you spend at home?
11. What do you enjoy doing when you are at home?
12. Do you need an extra room or an available space that can be converted into a home office?
13. How much (if any) effect will a home's physical location make on your buying decision?

By answering these and other questions that come to mind as you go through this discovery process, you'll know more about important features your house must have such as:

1. Number of bedrooms and bathrooms
2. Accessibility options
3. Lot size
4. Proximity to amenities such as schools, churches, shopping centers, entertainment and recreation facilities, and medical facilities
5. Minimum square footage

Why Do You Want to Own a Home?

In our experience, this is the one question potential buyers consider the least. They may know they are tired of their rent money being used to purchase more property for their landlord, or they hope the tax benefits will offset the higher monthly payment of a mortgage.

However, they usually have not thought about some of these other aspects of home ownership:

1. How important is owning a pet or being able to make changes to your living environment?
2. How important are hobbies like gardening, growing flowers, or landscaping?

3. Will you own real estate to provide yourself with housing and shelter, or do you want investment and rental properties to increase your cash flow and net worth?
4. How important are issues like freedom of individual expression, privacy and security to you?
5. Are you living at home or with a roommate?
6. Do you want more freedom?
7. How interested are you in acquiring an asset that will probably appreciate over time?
8. How would it change your life to stop waiting for the property owner to fix or to maintain your residence or to stop increasing your rent?

What Do You Do?

You also need to know how you spend your time both on and off the job. Notate your responses to the following and include the answers to any additional questions that come to mind.

1. What is your occupation?
2. Do you go to an office or job site or work from home?
3. Do you travel for business, commute or stay local?
4. Are you self-employed or work for an employer?
5. Is your job seasonal?
6. What is your income?
7. What changes in income do you project in two years, five years and ten years?
8. Are you considering a career change?
9. What do you do for leisure?
10. What are your hobbies or interests?

Where Do You Want to Live?

In addition to discovering whom you are and what you do, you need to look at where you want to live. As you work through this discovery process, you'll find some of the sections may begin to overlap.

For instance, where you want to live may be closely linked to your occupation or other aspects of your life. If you find yourself thinking of other questions relating to a previous section, just go back there and jot down the extra information. The more you know about your desires and lifestyle, the happier you'll be in your new home.

Ask yourself:

1. Where do you work?
2. How far are you willing to commute?
3. Is public transportation a necessity?
4. Where are the closest schools?
5. How is their quality and reputation?
6. Do they provide transportation or will you need to factor that into your search?
7. Where is the nearest preschool or day care center?
8. How close do you need to be to shopping centers and grocery stores?
9. Where are your healthcare, vision or dental providers located?
10. How close to them would you like to be?
11. Where are the nearest community or cultural amenities?
12. Where do you want to live in the next 5, 10 or 30 years?

What Kind of Home Do You Want?

Now that you have the framework of your search criteria identified, you can begin to fill in the smaller details. In this section, we want to encourage you to continue your discovery process and narrow down the type of houses for which you will be looking.

Some revealing questions to ask might be:

1. Do you want a detached, single family home, or would you be more comfortable in closer proximity to neighbors in a duplex or townhome?
2. How important is community to you? If you're extremely social and love to interact with others on an almost daily

basis, would a common interest property like a condominium be best for you?

3. Do you want to build your own home so you'll have more control over the design and amenities, or would you rather choose a modular (prefabricated) home?

4. Is a pre-owned home acceptable, or are you determined to buy a brand-new, never-lived-in house?

After you've completed this section, you can add your home type criteria to your previous data. In the next section, we'll help you decide what amenities are essential for you to get the most enjoyment from living in your new home.

The Icing on the Cake

So far, we've discussed why you want a house, what your lifestyle needs are, and the kind of house you want. Now let's talk about the fun stuff! What extras and luxuries do you want included in your home purchase?

1. How important are other building structures like garages, storage buildings, workshops and so forth?

2. Is the lack of such a structure a deal-breaker for you?

3. Would you like an indoor or outdoor pool with your home or other features such as a hot tub?

4. How important is access to services like high-speed data lines or state maintained roads?

5. Do you need a bonus room like a finished room over the garage (FROG) or a great room, or would the additional space be just another room to clean?

6. What type of heating, air conditioning, and water do you want? (For instance, well water versus city water.)

7. Do you own your appliances like a stove, dishwasher and refrigerator, or is it important to have those included as a part of the home buying package?

Add the amenities to your list in addition to any other items or must-haves that came to mind while you were working through this exercise.

We know this has been a long process thus far, so why not treat yourself to a quick coffee break, and then we'll examine the necessary soul-searching you must do to create the ultimate dream house wish list.

How Will You Achieve Your Dream?

This is the most important area of focus because buying a home is one of the largest purchases many people ever make. You do not want to be carried away by emotion and find yourself married to a home you cannot afford.

Ask yourself these tough questions now to avoid a foreclosure or bankruptcy down the road:

1. How important is it to you to get a low interest rate on your loan?
2. Can you afford to buy the interest down upfront via points to lower your monthly payments?
3. How many open lines of credit do you already have?
4. What is the total amount of your outstanding credit obligations?
5. How is your credit rating?
6. If it is poor, how can you improve it?
7. How large a down payment can you afford?
8. Where will you get the money?
9. How have you paid your debts in the past?
10. What does your credit history look like?
11. How long has your credit line been open?
12. How much new credit do you have?
13. How will you afford your monthly payments?
14. What would happen if you lost your job, contracted an expensive illness, or suffered a disastrous accident or calamity?
15. How much total debt are you carrying?

Make Your List, Check It Twice

Congratulations! You've completed your journey to the final step: incorporating all the data you've collected into a dream house wish list. We know it seems like a long process, and to be honest, if we could have worked with you during this discovery process, it would have taken a couple of hours to figure out why you want to buy a home, where you want to live, and sort out all the other vital information.

However, once you are settled into the home of your dreams, you'll be glad you invested a tiny amount of time on the front end to gain a high level of satisfaction on the back end.

With this valuable data, you can create a wish list for your next home based on your lifestyle, your occupation, and your likes and dislikes.

By thinking about what you do want, you've also discovered what you don't want in your new home. You are ready to take the next step, which is to hire your real estate agent, take your wish list, and start shopping.

You've created a concise list of what you need and want in a home to share with your real estate agent. Knowing the specifics of what you are looking for in a house helps your agent do a better job of selecting the right properties to show you and saves you both time and money. Creating a wish list for your perfect home was a lot of fun, wasn't it?

4 – TYPES OF HOME LOANS

Chances are, you will need to borrow the money to purchase your home unless you have a very rich relative who will give you a loan. If you are fresh out of rich relations to help you out financially, you must become very familiar with the different types of loans for buying a house. Choosing the right loan can save you a tremendous amount of money over the life of the loan if it lowers your interest rate.

In addition, did you realize that if you pay off your mortgage early, you could save a tremendous amount of money by not having to pay the interest for the full term of the loan?

Buying a home comes with a host of available financing options, some of which can seem confusing. The following definitions for the types of home loans explain the various loans and the issuing agencies. These definitions help clear up any confusion whether you are trying to figure out the alphabet soup of housing agencies or decipher how a type of loan is structured.

Federal Housing Administration (FHA)

The Federal Housing Association offers mortgage insurance for loans issued through approved lenders in the United States and its territories. It insures mortgages on a variety of housing types including multifamily or single family homes. FHA loans differ from traditional loans in that they issue loans with 3.5 percent down.

It's important for the potential homeowner to understand that FHA and VA "loans" are not loans that are made by the government. The individual lenders loan the money; the government insures the loan. Once the mortgage broker originates the loan, it is immediately marketed to the secondary mortgage market in most cases.

Veteran's Guaranteed Loan (VA)

A VA loan is similar to an FHA loan, but differs in that it is available only to US veterans and to veteran's family members that fall under a specific definition. A VA loan allows up to 103.15 percent financing, which means the veteran can borrow up to 103.15 percent of the purchase price.

Conventional (Conforming Loans)

A conforming loan is one that is the equivalent of or less than the highest loan limit allowable by the FHA. The FHA uses a formula to set the upper limit of allowable mortgage purchases.

A single family home has an upper limit of $417,000 in most parts of the country. Homes in HI, AK, GU and the VI (Virgin Islands) have $625,500 as a standard. High cost areas, such as parts of California, are allowed a limit exemption up to $625,500 for a single family home and $1,202,925 for a four-unit apartment building.

Most conventional loans require a larger down payment, which is typically 20% of the selling price.

Conventional (Non-conforming Loans)

A Government Sponsored Enterprise (GSE) such as the FHA does not insure these mortgages. As such, they do not conform to a maximum loan amount. These types of loans are available from a variety of lending institutions. This means the interest rates, terms and fees differ from lender to lender, making it imperative to shop various financial institutions in order to get the most favorable loan.

Seller Financing

With seller financing, the owner of a property provides the financing directly to the buyer with the property acting as the security for the loan. This benefits the buyer who cannot qualify for a mortgage from a lending institution. Typically, a binding agreement is drawn up that gives the seller the right to take back the property if the buyer defaults.

Municipal Grants

In the case of municipal grants, a municipality offers financial assistance to first time homebuyers, usually for purchasing a home in a designated area. The idea is to get people to move into homes in order to fill in vacant homes and keep a neighborhood free from blight. However, each municipality can issue grants as they see fit so terms will be different from city to city.

State Housing Programs

In general, state housing programs provide mortgage assistance for first time homebuyers who are considered low-to-moderate income earners. For example, in Virginia, individuals who are interested in this type of program would contact the Virginia Housing Development Authority for more information.

The idea is to help families get into stable housing by offering down payment and closing costs. Programs differ from state to state, so check your state's website before jumping into a home.

Home Equity Loans

Equity is available after the mortgage has been paid down, which creates a value "pocket" between the outstanding balance and the value of the house. For example, if a home is valued at $200,000 and the outstanding mortgage is $115,000, the difference creates $85,000 in equity.

In theory, a home equity loan can be taken out for $85,000, although the bank may prefer less be taken out to reduce their risk exposure. Regardless, when a homeowner exercises this option, he or she is using the equity (or cash value) of the property to get further financing.

Second Mortgages

These loans are literally a second mortgage taken out on a home although they are sometimes called a down payment loan if taken out at the time of purchase. Second mortgages are subordinate to the first mortgage, which means if financial issues arise, the first mortgage gets payment priority and the holder of the second mortgage potentially waits for payment.

Because the lending institute for the second mortgage is putting their funds at higher risk by placing themselves in a secondary position, an individual will usually pay a higher interest rate on this type of loan.

Decoding the Government Sponsored Enterprise (GSE)

Fannie Mae: Federal National Mortgage Association

A government sponsored enterprise (GSE) that provides funding to lenders instead of directly funding a homebuyer. Fannie Mae tends to focus on affordable housing initiatives. Homes are available through Fannie Mae via the HomePath program.

Freddie Mac: Federal Home Loan Mortgage Corporation

A GSE that purchases mortgages for investment and issues mortgage-related securities. Freddie Mac also provides mortgage funding to lenders and offers a variety of lending products.

Ginnie Mae: Government National Mortgage Association

A GSE that does not offer, buy or sell loans or mortgage-backed securities. Ginnie Mae guarantees mortgage lenders timely payment of principal and interest on mortgage-backed securities (MBSs) that are backed by federally insured loans.

Federal mortgage loan backers are the FHA, VA, Rural Housing Service (RHS) and the Office of Public and Indian Housing (PIH).

5 – FORMS OF HOME OWNERSHIP

In this chapter, we want to give you a basic overview of the various forms of home ownership. This helps you understand what your real estate professional or lender is referring to when they use the professional jargon that is sometimes incomprehensible to the nonprofessional.

Sole Ownership

In a sole ownership, or estate in severalty as it is also known, one person holds title to the property. This type of ownership is available to single and married persons or businesses.

In the case of married couples, depending on the regulations of the state in which they reside, one of them may have to relinquish dower, community property, or curtsey rights if a sole ownership status is desired.

An easy way to understand the "severalty" portion of this is to think of the term "severed". This type of ownership gives individuals the highest form of flexibility when it comes to the resale of the home because there are no co-owners to impede any decisions that are made regarding the property.

You can keep it, rent it, improve it, or sell it with impunity. No matter what you do with it, you have the freedom to act without any outside interference. On the downside, homebuyers should be aware that sole ownership is one of the most expensive types of ownership.

Tenant in Common

An easy way to remember the definition of a tenancy in common is to think of it as a unity or equality of possession between two or more owners who hold separate legal title to an undivided interest in the property.

No matter how many owners there are, each owns the entire property. No owner can restrict, impede or exclude another owner from the use and enjoyment of the property. If one (or more) of the owners sells their interest, the new owner becomes a tenant in common with the remaining owners.

There is no right of survivorship. In other words, the remaining owners do not automatically become the owners of the interest in the property of the deceased owner. Instead, the deceased owner's heirs become tenants in common with the surviving owners. Depending on personalities, lifestyles, cultural mores and so forth, this can be an agreeable or disagreeable arrangement for everyone involved.

Joint Tenancy

Four elements must be present in a joint tenancy, and they must operate in unity: time, title, interest and possession.

1. **Unity of time:** Each joint tenant acquires an interest in the property at the same time. No new joint tenants can be added.

2. **Unity of title:** The interests in the property must be acquired from the same source for all the joint tenants.

3. **Unity of interest:** The property is considered one single unit owned by all the joint tenants equally. No one joint tenant has a larger interest than another does.

4. **Unity of possession:** All the joint tenants own the entire property and are entitled to the unrestricted use and enjoyment of it.

On the surface, joint tenancy seems to make sense for married couples because of the right of survivorship. In the event of the death of one of the spouses, the property goes directly to the surviving spouse without having to pass through probate. The surviving spouse is then the sole owner.

In fact, joint tenancy is often referred to as the "poor man's will" because of this feature. However, because it only affects property rather than all the marital assets, it does not afford complete protection for the survivor. In addition, a spouse could enter into a joint tenancy with someone other than his or her spouse. In that case, upon his or her death, the property would pass to the surviving joint tenant rather than the surviving spouse.

Unlike a sole ownership, only humans can enter into a joint tenancy; businesses and corporations cannot.

Tenancy by the entirety

Tenancy by the entirety is the most common form of ownership and is designed for married couples. A fifth unity is added to the four mentioned earlier to form a tenancy by the entirety: **unity of person**.

In plain English, for legal purposes, the husband and wife are considered as a single, indivisible unit.

Tenancy in common includes the right of survivorship, as the surviving spouse becomes the sole owner upon the death of the other spouse. While both spouses are alive, neither has a disposable interest in the property. If the couples should divorce, they become tenants in common.

Community property

For legal purposes, in states that recognize community property, the husband and wife are deemed to have contributed equally and jointly to the marriage. They share equally in any property acquired during the marriage and hold a one-half interest.

Separate property

Separate property is any property acquired by either party prior to the marriage or after the marriage by inheritance or gift. It may also include any property bought with separate funds.

Except for separate property, any properties purchased after the marriage are deemed community property. As such, each person would have a one-half interest in them and could convey them or mortgage them in any fashion that suited them.

Because the laws governing community property vary from state to state, readers are advised to seek legal advice for the specifics of the laws pertaining to their state of residence.

6 – GET YOUR FINANCIAL HOUSE IN ORDER

What do you need to know if you want to raise your credit score quickly? After all, a high credit score gives you a higher possibility of getting your credit applications approved.

High credit scores such as a FICO score of 760 or higher typically mean you pay a lower interest rate when you borrow money.

What's Your Number?

The top three credit reporting agencies in America are TransUnion, Equifax and Experian. Each offers consumers a free copy of their credit report once a year.

However, if you want to know your credit score, what you are really looking for is your FICO score, and you may have to pay for this information. In addition, be aware that these three agencies may or may not sell those scores to consumers.

How to Raise Credit Scores

So, how can you improve your credit score?

First, check your credit report for any inaccuracies in your past credit history and all associated pertinent data. Entries on your credit report are a part of the method used to calculate your credit score, so disputing any errors promptly is very important in maintaining a high score.

Scan the document for any reports of your account being sent to a collection agency or negative statements such as "paid charge-off," "late payments," "did not pay as agreed," "paid but derogatory" and so forth.

Disputing requirements may vary among the top three credit reporting agencies so be sure you understand their guidelines and submit your request in their required format to have any inaccurate information revised or deleted. Your dispute request should be in writing (not verbal.) Ask for a written response to your request. Correcting inaccurate data is a good way to raise your credit score.

Pay Your Debts on Time

Second: If you pay your credit obligations on time, you will rarely have to worry about a low credit score as missed payments are another factor that affect how high or low your score will be. Making your payments on time and keeping your credit balances low are the two best ways to keep your credit score high and your record clean.

Credit reporting agencies look at the balances on both installment and credit card obligations when calculating a credit score. To get the highest score, keep the balances on the credit cards paid down or pay them off in full each month. Having several lines of open credit card accounts with balances that are almost at the maximum available credit limit will usually result in getting a lower score.

Applying for too many new credit accounts can affect your credit score as well. Too many open lines of credit or too many accounts opened relatively close together can cause your credit score to be lowered.

While many people like to have several credit cards available so they can better plan their purchases or take advantage of customer loyalty or reward programs, having too many open credit card accounts is perceived as a negative by most credit reporting agencies and may cause your score to be lowered.

Mix Your Credit Portfolio

Third: Maintain a mix of credit obligations. If the only open credit lines you have are for credit cards, it could result in a lower score. Paying responsibly on a long-term installment loan such as a car or mortgage payment demonstrates your history as a credit-worthy individual. Paying off your credit card debt raises your credit score faster than paying off installment loans because it closes the gap between the available credit limit and the balance owed.

Why Credit Scores Matter

Lenders use credit scores to determine their risk when extending credit to a borrower. These scores help them assess an individual's ability to pay off the obligation on time. Credit institutions make money by extending credit to borrowers so making sure they only lend money to people who are responsible enough to pay them on time is a smart business move.

By analyzing your credit score, they can make a calculated assessment of the risk of approving a credit application. If they feel that the risk of default is too high, they will reject the credit application.

Benefits of High Credit Scores

While a high credit score does not guarantee you would not default on a debt obligation, it does make you an attractive prospect when you apply for credit. Lenders want borrowers who they feel would pay their debts so they use the credit score as a basis for determining your credit risk. Historically speaking, they know there is a lower risk of default when lending to individuals with higher credit scores, and this knowledge translates into a better chance for the approval of your credit applications.

If you are planning on making a major purchase in the near future such as a new car or home, you may want to take steps to raise your credit score now before you apply for a loan. Assessing your current credit indebtedness is an important step in the process of deciding how much mortgage (and home) you can afford.

One of the confusing things for the first time homebuyer is deciphering unfamiliar real estate industry jargon such as prequalification or preapproval. Are these terms synonymous or radically different? Is one preferable to the other and if so, which is the best choice?

Here we explain both terms in plain English and provide you with other facts to help you decide if you should prequalify for a mortgage or opt to get preapproval for a home loan. You may also want to ask your real estate agent for advice.

Balancing the Financial Scales

A good word picture for "prequalify" is a balance scale. In the prequalification process, you weigh factors such as your gross monthly income and obligations against the purchase price and additional expenses of home ownership. Obviously, if the scales are tipped dangerously high on the expense side, you may or may not want to take the risk of committing to the largest purchase of your life.

Here is what happens in the prequalification process:

Step one: Calculate your gross monthly income from all sources before any deductions are made. Some lenders refer to this as your net worth.

Step two: Calculate all your monthly expenses. These are your net liabilities, and these are subtracted from your net worth to calculate your net monthly income.

Step three: Determine the loan term, average percentage rate (at current mortgage interest rates), and local property tax percentages.

For step four: Either you or the lender will calculate the debt to income ratio. This simply means comparing all outstanding debt to all available income to determine a percentage. (Turn back to Chapter 1, pages 5 to 7, for a refresher on this subject if you would like.) The gold standard in the mortgage/real estate industry for a conventional loan is 28/36.

To finish the process, your lender prepares a prequalification letter that you can show the seller. It is important to note that the letter simply states a loan amount for which you may be able to qualify.

Prequalify or Preapproval for a Mortgage?

Prequalification is not the same as preapproval for a mortgage. The lender may or may not pull a credit report to check your credit history. He or she makes no commitment to approve you for a mortgage.

While taking the step to prequalify for a home mortgage loan is better than not taking this step, if you want to be in the best position to negotiate with sellers, go one step further and get a mortgage preapproval.

When you prequalify for a home loan, you have taken some of the basic steps for a mortgage preapproval. However, you need to get more documentation together for your preapproval meeting with your lender.

The exact documentation you must provide depends on the individual lender's guidelines, but at a minimum, you should expect to provide:

- W2 forms (2-year minimum)
- Recent pay stub
- Tax returns (2-year minimum)
- Purchase offer (if you have made one)
- Net worth statement (this is necessary for self-employed individuals)
- Bank statements (3-month minimum)
- Verification of investments and other income sources
- Verification of all debts

If you are depending on another person's income to help you qualify for a loan, you must provide documentation for all of the above for the other person as well. If you are self-employed, be prepared to show solid evidence of profitability for at least three consecutive years.

The Rest of the Preapproval Process

The lender will expect you to fill out a loan application, and there may or may not be an application fee. Typically, if your loan application is denied, your fee is forfeited.

The loan approval process varies so much from lender to lender that it is difficult to give you a specific timeframe. However, you should expect to wait anywhere from two or three days to several weeks for a decision. If you are approved for the loan, the lender will give you a preapproval letter to show the seller.

The preapproval letter is not a guarantee of a loan as your situation could change dramatically during your home search. Most preapprovals are for a specified time, and you might not find your home in that timeframe.

However, having a preapproval letter shows lenders, sellers and real estate agents you are serious about home ownership. Almost anyone can get a prequalification, as it is possible to prequalify online with a few clicks of the mouse. To get a preapproval, you do have to invest some time and effort. So, what is the best choice for your situation? Prequalify or preapproval for a mortgage?

7 – INTERVIEW AND HIRE YOUR AGENT

For most people, buying a home is the biggest investment they will ever make. Finding the best-qualified real estate professional to help them make that purchase is crucial. While there are never any guarantees in life, if you take the time to ask potential agents the following questions, you improve your odds of making the best hiring decision.

1. Are they Realtors® or real estate agents?

A real estate agent is any duly licensed person registered with the state. A Realtor® goes a step further and belongs to three major associations at the local, state and national level. Whereas the real estate agent and the Realtor® both adhere to a certain code of ethics, the perception is Realtors® adhere to a stricter set of ethics. Realtors® have the ability to access the home listings of real estate professionals worldwide through their associations.

2. What other professional certifications or designations do they hold?

The GRI, or graduate of real estate institute, certification is good, and it gives any agent a broader understanding of their duties and responsibilities. In addition, any agent holding a broker's license, whether he is serving as a managing broker, broker/owner, or associate broker, is exposed to a certain amount of additional education.

3. How long have they been in the real estate industry?

Some agents of one to three years experience are extremely effective, but with others, it may take longer for them to attain that level of proficiency. You can tactfully ask them about their experience and what their sales are tied to such as residential, commercial, land, farms and so forth. Tie their expertise to your wants and needs.

4. Is this their full-time or part-time job?

If you hire a part-time real estate person, be it a real estate agent or Realtor®, we respectfully suggest you should expect to receive part-time service. An individual who works full time and earns a living in the real estate profession provides full time service and dedication to you as their client.

5. What methods do they use to find dream homes for their clients?

Firstly, mostly, and lastly, they should listen actively to what potential buyers tell them and try to show them products tailored to their wishes and needs. It really hinges on listening instead of trying to shove something down the client's throat just make a sale.

6. Will they present your offers personally?

Any good agent can and will do this. They will present all offers; not just the ones they think will be accepted.

7. How will they communicate with you during the purchase offer and negotiation process?

A good agent communicates with you day by day and hour by hour. Are you an email-text-fax type person or do you prefer the more traditional phone call? It's important to match your agent's communication style to yours.

8. Will they be present at the home inspection, the termite inspection, and the closing?

Any responsible agent is present at all these functions. Some will question this and say, "Well, do they really need to be at all of them?"

Our belief and philosophy is that while they do not have to be at all these functions, they will be there if they are serving their client's best interests.

9. Will they allow you to review documents such as the buyer's broker agreement and the buyer disclosure or consult with an attorney before they ask you to sign them?

Absolutely! Although the quantities of documentation these days are greater than ever before and can be overwhelming to the uninitiated, it is important that you understand what each one means and how it applies to you. This is the most significant purchase you will ever make so you need to do your due diligence and be sure you understand all the fine print and legalese.

10. How will they help you find the other professionals you need to complete your home purchase such as a lender, closing attorney, title company, and home inspector?

The true professional has developed a list of the reliable and efficient ones by trial and error.

11. Are they buyer's agents, seller's agents, or dual agents?

Any agent who works for you should identify his or her agency affiliation at the beginning before they do the first ancillary work for you. Before they take any action on your behalf, they should disclose their allegiance; for instance, I am working for the seller, or I am a dual agent. Full disclosure is imperative.

12. What is their fee?

At the beginning of your relationship, the agent should be able to quote you an exact fee, and he or she will probably quote it as a percentage. He or she is quoting his or her fee, not what other agents or other companies expect to receive.

13. How many clients do they handle in a year?

Some of your bigger producers handle fewer clients because they cater to a higher priced clientele. You may not necessarily want a high volume producer; you may want someone more seasoned who handles more quality clients. This type of agent devotes more time to your purchase.

Alternatively, you may want a mover or shaker who is familiar with major metropolitan areas and does lots of business because he or she is more likely to find what you need.

Age differences come into play as well. Older clients may prefer an agent who is closer to their own age bracket and operates differently, while younger clients may very well prefer one of the "now crowd."

14. What was their volume; in other words, their market prices for their sales listings last year.

As we mentioned before, sales volume or the tenure of an agent does not always give a true picture of expertise. An agent working in a low-end market may have to sell more to achieve the same amount of volume than one in a high-end market does.

Oftentimes, agents develop their own niche markets. Some may specialize in farm and rural properties while others do the majority of their business in the resort or condominium industry. This affects the number of clients they handle but does not reflect on the quality of the agent.

15. Will they provide you with a list of six references from their last 10 sales?

Any good agent should be willing to provide you with as many references as you want: professional, personal or otherwise.

16. Has a client ever filed a complaint against them?

Any agent should be willing to disclose this information and not be offended if you ask. If they have been convicted of a felony, then they should not hold a real estate license.

Even if they have never done anything illegal, has their abrasive personality or lack of social skills prompted a client to complain about them to a broker? It is important for you to feel comfortable with and trust your real estate agent.

17. What is their level of experience with short sales, auctions and foreclosures?

Many agents do not handle these types of sales; it is important to know this up front. If you want that type of purchase, you need to know if they would show you those properties. As Chuck says, "Myself, I won't fool with one because I'm not sure I'll live long enough to get one closed."

18. Will you be working with just them or do they have a team or a personal assistant?

You want to know if they will give you individual attention or hand you off to someone else.

19. What awards and recognition have they won?

I think we all know the true value of a lifetime's accumulation of plaques, trophies and awards. Just don't try to buy a cup of coffee with them!

A better question to ask is, "In what esteem are they held by their peers, associates and clients?" An agent can be highly productive but not get along well with the crowd.

20. How do they stay current with what is happening in the real estate industry?

Good agents take advantage of seminars, retreats, association sponsored meetings, and any opportunities for continuing education. Whether you are a real estate agent or realtor, you must take a predetermined amount of continuing education classes to maintain your real estate or broker's license.

In my case (Chuck's), although I am not a managing broker, I have to have 24 hours of continuing education every two years to maintain my license. The courses can be taken in a classroom, by correspondence courses, or online. A sales agent needs 16 hours of continuing education.

By now, you should have a good idea of how well the real estate professional you are interviewing has done in the business and how satisfied the other clients have been.

In addition, you've observed body language, speech patterns, and personality traits so you have a good overall picture of the individual. If you are satisfied you have found the right person, congratulations! Sign the contract and get ready to house hunt.

However, if you are not completely satisfied, you are probably wise to do a few more interviews before you make your selection.

Here are some final questions to help you solidify your decision:

21. How quickly do they respond to client phone calls and emails?

A quick turnaround is very important, and good communication with clients is necessary.

22. To which trade or professional organizations do they belong?

Most agents belong to the National Association of Realtors (NAR), and in Virginia, we have the Virginia Association of Realtors (VAR) and the MLS. Belonging to organizations provides agents with better exposure to the widest range of educational and professional resources.

23. What is their guarantee or pledge of service?

Most franchises or agencies have their unique guarantee or pledge. However, the bottom line with any good agent is the desire to make a living selling real estate. To make a good living, they have to do a good job and satisfy their clients.

24. What is their level of intimate knowledge of your target neighborhood?

It's not a good idea to work with an agent who does not know the geography of your desired neighborhood. Identifying the makeup of your target neighborhood is a key part of creating your dream house list.

25. What is their level of comfort and familiarity with newer technology like the Internet?

Maybe a high tech mover and shaker is the kind of individual with whom you feel most comfortable. On the other hand, a low tech, old-fashioned foot soldier who does not mind patrolling on foot and searching every nook and cranny for those hidden treasures might suit you better.

There is a new certification for agents who are proficient with using the Internet as a sales tool. It's called E-Pro, and if that's your thing, you should look for an agent with expertise in this area. These agents can take you to listings and pull up all the pertinent information from MLS on a laptop computer.

Now, the old "hard-headed" agents like me (Chuck) just will not do this because they do not want anything to take place in the car that will break the train of thought.

Just Say No

Never, ever hire friends or family as your real estate agent. It is easier and less painful to fire a stranger. This is the biggest single purchase made in your lifetime, and you want to invest more than thirty minutes in interviewing and hiring the person to help you make that acquisition.

For example, if you want to buy a television, you want one built by a professional. You do not buy all the parts and try to build one yourself. While you could obtain an engineering degree and eventually build a television, it is not worth your time and effort, and neither is trying to be your own real estate agent in the hopes of saving a few dollars.

Would you rather have a brain surgeon do your surgery or a real estate agent do your surgery? Would you rather a car mechanic fix your car or an accountant? Would you prefer to buy a television or build it yourself? Obviously, you want the most highly trained professional you can find to be your partner on your biggest lifetime purchase.

Avoid Personality Clashes

One of the most important steps in buying a home you will enjoy for a lifetime is to find a real estate agent whose personality and communication style meshes well with yours. That's why it is in your best interests to interview several agents before you make your final selection.

Here's an example of what can go wrong when personalities clash:

There was an extremely successful real estate agent in our town and her sales method was as follows:

She would make a very hurried assessment of her potential buyer's needs and select three properties she thought would suit. She would attempt to cram one of those properties down their throats. Even though she was successful, needless to say, she made many people angry and lost numerous clients.

Over time she developed such a negative reputation, she eventually left the business. Some might say how fortunate for her clientele she decided to pursue other employment options.

As you can guess, working with this type of personality could mean you end up saddled with a house that doesn't meet your needs, and you will hate every minute of your life there. Unless this is your style, avoid this personality type.

Your Real Estate Agent's Role

What can you expect your real estate agent to do for you in addition to taking you to view houses in a target neighborhood?

Your Realtor® helps with tasks like these listed below but may also offer you many more services over and above these common ones:

- Assess a property's long-term true value.
- Identify potential problems in an area such as high traffic volumes or proximity to hazards like open bodies of water.
- Prepare and present your purchase offer.
- Negotiate and close the home sale.
- Act as your liaison with other professionals such as the loan officer, home inspector, appraiser, surveyor and so forth.

How to Make Your Real Estate Agent Love You

We spent a lot of time talking about questions to ask a potential real estate agent so you can make the best choice of qualifications and personalities to complement your own.

However, as real estate professionals ourselves, we would be remiss if we concluded this chapter without including a few tips on your role as the buyer, and our recommendations for how you can facilitate a smooth transaction on your end of the partnership.

1. **Be respectful:** Remember your real estate agent is paid by the sale and not by the hour. Be respectful of his or her time and do not ask for second or third visits to a home in which you are not seriously interested.

2. **Be realistic:** Good agents present any offer a client makes, but that does not mean they should be put in the position of presenting an offer that is obviously an unrealistic low-ball offer.

3. **Honor the respective roles:** As the buyer, the real estate agent does work for you. However, that relationship does not give you the right to negotiate directly with the seller to try to obtain a lower price or otherwise manipulate the costs involved in buying the home. Let the agent do their job and you do yours.

4. **Be decisive:** Some prospects turn home viewing into a mini-career in and of itself, and while they are always willing to look at another property, they are never willing to make a commitment. If you are not serious about buying a house just yet, do not tie up the agent's time with window-shopping.

5. **Be positive:** Work from a positive rather than negative point of view. Let's face it, the perfect property or home does not exist, and you can easily find fault with any house. However, if you weigh the advantages over the disadvantages, it is much easier to make an unbiased decision. Your real estate agent will help you with this process.

6. **Return calls promptly:** Communication is a big factor in keeping a real estate transaction moving smoothly. Your agent may be calling to let you know about a vital piece of documentation that is missing or an additional expense that could be looming.

7. **Complete paperwork:** There is a tremendous amount of document verification to do before a home loan is approved and a real estate transaction finalized. Do your part by completing and returning any documentation quickly.

8. **Listen to your agent:** While this may or may not be an apples-to-apples comparison, buying your first home is similar to having your first baby. Everyone has an opinion to share, but not everyone agrees your healthcare professional or real estate agent is handling your affairs appropriately. After all, when Aunt Sally had her baby or Uncle John bought his home…you can probably finish this scenario for yourself. Friends and family mean well, but your agent is the expert.

The point is you invested time and effort in selecting the real estate professional in whom you had the most confidence and trust. Follow his or her advice and you will be packing and preparing to move into that new home in the shortest possible time.

8 – VIEW HOMES AND MAKE OFFERS

Now that you done the hard part, it is time to have some fun. One of the most exciting steps in the home buying process is viewing and choosing the best home for you.

Things to Do Before Viewing Homes

Be prepared with your checklist for home buying you created by following the directions in Chapter 3. The purpose of making a checklist is so you can give your real estate agent very specific information about the type of home and community you want.

At a minimum, know your target neighborhood, the type of home, how much home and mortgage payment you can afford, and the date you would like to move into your new home.

If you want to make the home buying process faster and more efficient, you might also want to prequalify for a home loan. If you skipped over that section earlier, you can find out everything you need to know in Chapter 6.

While a prequalification is not a guarantee you can obtain funding for your future home, it does make you stand out from the rest of the potential buyers in today's buyers' market and marks you as a serious prospect.

Armed with the vital information on your dream house list, your real estate professional can quickly identify some target homes and schedule appointments for you to view them. Once you find the perfect home, he or she will help you write up your purchase offer.

However, it has been our experience that most homebuyers have many questions about the purchase offer process. Here are our answers to some of the most frequently asked questions.

Purchase Offers FAQs

Why do you advise your clients to make written purchase offers?

Verbal offers are just are not appropriate because the seller has no way of knowing if a prospect is serious about the purchase. Put an offer to purchase agreement down on paper and back it up with good faith money.

Here is a perfect example of why you do not want to make a verbal contract; an oral contract is legal in the state of Virginia but it is very unenforceable. In our opinions, an oral contract is only as good as the paper on which it is **not** written.

How does one go about putting the purchase offer together so it has the highest chance of acceptance?

First, you have to determine the offer price and many factors determine that. For instance, a good real estate agent will give you a current market analysis, which lists comparables of what has sold in the area.

Second, the seller's motivation is always a crucial factor. The more you know about the seller and how motivated he or she is, the better equipped you are to structure your purchase offer.

Third, be reasonable and make a serious offer. You do not want to put out a ridiculously low offer that no one could accept. Demonstrate to the seller that you are a willing, ready and viable prospect by offering a realistic amount of good faith money (also referred to as earnest money).

Fourth, limit the number of contingencies tied to the purchase offer. Be ready and willing to close in an appropriate amount of time.

Fifth, make sure your agent is representing you because if you are dealing with an agent that is representing the seller, his fiduciary is to the seller, which means he or she is working to get the best possible deal for the seller.

Two Scenarios to Consider

Let's say a seller is looking at two different purchase offers. One of them is for full asking price but it is loaded with contingencies ("what if" clauses). The good faith money is minimal and chances of a smooth, quick closing are low.

On the other hand, the seller has an offer to purchase agreement that is a few thousand dollars less than the asking price. However, there are just a few contingencies, the amount of the good faith money is high, the buyer is prequalified for the mortgage, and the likelihood of a speedy, efficient close is good.

Most sellers will opt to either counter or accept the second offer over the full price offer because there is a better chance of finalizing the transaction with a minimum of effort and hassle. Time is money for everyone in the home buying process.

What is your idea of a reasonable amount to offer as good faith money?

It depends on the amount of the purchase price, of course. For instance, on a property with a million dollar price tag, we would want to see an earnest money offer of several thousand dollars.

Some people plunk down one or two hundred dollars and think that amount is acceptable, but in the back of their minds, they are willing to risk walking away from the deposit if necessary because it is such a small amount. In our area (Virginia), on the average residential purchase, the average deposit would be three to five hundred dollars.

Who actually writes the offer to purchase agreement, the buyer or the buyer's agent?

In our area, the buyer's representative writes the purchase offer in the form of a contract. The completed agreement is presented (ideally, in person) to the selling agent. A good buyer's agent will ask to be present when the selling agent presents the purchase offer to the seller.

While the seller's agent does not have to permit the other agent to be present, most allow this as a professional courtesy to a colleague. We make it a rule to ask to be present at any presentation that involves our clients.

If there needs to be any negotiation over the terms of the offer, the seller's agent may ask to confer privately with their clients, and we have no problem with this. We are always willing to wait elsewhere while they discuss their options, especially if it means our offer has a better chance of being accepted.

Note to real estate professionals: There is an easy solution if you run up against a seller's agent who refuses to let you be present when he or she presents your client's offer to the seller. Ask the individual to make a trial presentation to you.

This ensures that when the other agent presents the offer to the seller, the presentation does not include any items to which your buyer would not agree. In essence, the seller's agent is "selling" your offer to the seller. The moral to this story is any real estate professional worth his salt will try to be present at any major event in the sales process such as closing, home inspection, and so forth.

What does the flow of the process of making an offer to purchase look like?

1. The buyer and real estate agent negotiate the terms the buyer wants to include in the purchase offer.
2. The real estate agent writes the offer in the form of a contract to purchase. After the buyer approves it, the real estate agent presents it to the seller's agent.
3. The seller's agent presents it to the seller.
4. At this stage of the purchase offer process, **one of three** things will happen:

- The seller accepts the purchase offer as presented.
- The seller makes a counter offer to the buyer.
- The seller rejects the purchase offer.

Let us interject here that a good real estate agent will not allow the seller to reject an offer outright unless it is just very unrealistic. These agents look for ways to construct a counter offer that protects the seller's interests while offering a way to move the transaction toward a close.

If the seller counters an offer, then the process just reverses itself: the seller's agent presents the counteroffer to the buyer's agent, who then presents it to the buyer. The wisdom of the seller's agent in allowing us to be there when the original offer is presented to the seller is now evident because if he asks to be included when we present the counteroffer to the buyer, we am more inclined to say yes.

What happens after the offer is accepted?

All the necessary documentation is completed, the financing is secured by obtaining a mortgage, and a time is set for closing the transaction. If you prequalified for a mortgage, that prequalification must be converted into a commitment from the lender to extend you financing for the purchase price of the home if the home and you, the buyer, meet all the loan underwriting guidelines. Your real estate agent will help you find the appropriate professional to help you with the mortgage process such as a mortgage banker or mortgage broker.

9 – THE MORTGAGE PROCESS AND FAQS

If you are ready to move ahead with the process, then understanding the differences between a mortgage banker and a mortgage broker is easy if you use word pictures to help you visual their roles.

The mortgage banker lends money and often services the resulting loan by collecting payments and so forth. Picture an individual with stacks of money on a desk, and you'll have no trouble remembering that you need a mortgage banker to get the funding for your mortgage.

The mortgage broker, on the other hand, does not lend money. He or she is like the person who arranges a marriage; so in essence, the mortgage broker brings together borrower and lender to create a "marriage" that results in a mortgage for the borrower and a commission for the mortgage banker.

The mortgage broker pockets a finder's fee, and everybody lives happily ever after (we hope!). Picture a beaming bride, a nervous bridegroom, and the officiating individual, and you'll always be able to differentiate the mortgage broker from the mortgage banker.

A mortgage banker is more likely to want to sell the types of home loans offered by his or her employer. He or she does not have much flexibility because of the company's requirements. On the other hand, the mortgage broker has many sources of mortgage money and can shop for the financing that best suits your situation.

We hope this brief and somewhat humorous explanation of how to tell the difference between these two key figures in the home search process is helpful.

We (the authors) are real estate experts and so far, we have shared with you the knowledge gained from years of working with clients just like you. However, as good as our knowledge of the real estate industry is, we are not financial experts nor do we pretend to be.

Our belief is your best source of information about the mortgage process and the best type of financing for your home purchase comes from your real estate professional and your loan officer.

As we mentioned earlier, your real estate professional will recommend a lender based on the knowledge and expertise gained through years of working with other industry professionals.

If you followed the instructions in Chapter 7 for interviewing and hiring your agent, then you have done your due diligence and made a good choice. It's time to trust your judgment and let your agent hold your hand through the mortgage process.

Mortgage FAQs

Choosing the best type of financing can make home buying seem complicated and confusing. Sometimes simply being able to decode the mortgage "jargon" is a tremendous help. For instance, what is a jumbo loan or a conventional mortgage?

We realize you may still have unanswered questions, so in the section below you will find answers to the most common questions our clients have asked us about mortgages or the loan process.

How do I know (or understand) the types of financing for my mortgage?

Most homebuyers opt for either a 30- or a 15-year conventional, FHA or VA loan. You need to decide which loan term best suits your circumstances and conforms to the loan's underwriting guidelines. For instance, not everyone can qualify for a VA or FHA loan because of the guidelines.

Next, evaluate the pros and cons of an adjustable rate mortgage versus a fixed rate mortgage.

Briefly, with a fixed rate mortgage, your monthly mortgage payment is a set amount, which makes budgeting easier. The monthly mortgage payment on an adjustable rate mortgage will fluctuate as the rate changes, so budgeting your expenses is not as simple. Your lender will give advice as to which mortgage product is best based on his or her experience, but ultimately the decision is yours.

What is an unconventional mortgage product?

These alternative loan programs are designed for individuals who do not qualify for a conventional mortgage. Some common unconventional loans are interest only loans or jumbo loans.

In an **interest only loan**, you pay only the interest on the loan (not the principal) for a predetermined number of years. At the end of that period, you begin to pay down the principal. The benefit is a lower payment in the beginning, but the disadvantage is you do not curtail the principal so you are not building any cash value, or equity, in the property. Building equity is one of the reasons for buying your home instead of renting.

A **jumbo mortgage** is a loan for which the amount being financed is more than the top amount set by the Government Sponsored Enterprises (GSE). If a mortgage is for more than the maximum amount set by the GSE guidelines, it is classified as a jumbo loan.

While this may seem like a good way to get a more expensive house, keep in mind the interest rates on jumbo loans may be significantly higher or the lender may require you to make a larger down payment.

We hope this information clarifies what lenders and real estate agents mean when they talk about conventional and unconventional mortgages. Now, let's look at some other questions that may come up during the financing phase of the home buying process.

Do 40-year mortgage loans make monthly home payments more affordable, or are they just another financial trap for potential homebuyers?

Chuck says: The alleged advantage of a longer-term mortgage like this is you pay a lower monthly payment because your thirty-year loan is amortized over an additional 10 years.

However, most 40-year mortgages include a balloon payment at the end of thirty years. If you cannot pay off the remaining balance, you have to hope you can refinance the loan. Since there is no way to predict what interest rates will be in the future, you could find yourself paying a much higher interest rate when you refinance the loan.

Because of this, many individuals choose an interest only loan as an alternative to get a similar low payment schedule. The difference between the two is with the 40-year mortgage you build equity in the property whereas on an interest only loan there is no equity buildup.

The best reason for considering 40-year mortgage loans is you feel confident you will not move or relocate during the life of the mortgage. Because of the cyclic nature of the real estate market, if you had to sell during a downturn in the market, you could end up taking a substantial financial loss.

(**Authors' note**: At the time this book was written, some jumbo loans were still available. This information is deemed reliable but no warranties are expressed or implied.)

What is earnest money?

Earnest money, which can be referred to as upfront money or good faith money, is a deposit paid upfront to legitimize the contract.

What happens to my earnest money if the deal falls through?

If you have complied with all the provisions of the contract, and the deal falls through, your money is refunded.

Is purchasing a home warranty necessary?

Chuck says: No. I do not personally recommend purchasing a home warranty, but if I were to suggest one, I would advise the person to find out what the deductible is, what the warranty covers, and so forth.

What is the advantage of a 15-year mortgage? How about a 30-year mortgage?

With a 15-year mortgage, you pay less interest and build equity faster, but the downside is you have a higher payment. The flip side is that with a 30-year mortgage, you make lower payments but you pay more interest and build equity slower. While there are longer-term loans available such as a 40-year mortgage, each buyer must do his or her due diligence before committing to any loan contract.

How much money should I put down on my house?

Pay as large an amount as you can afford. Most conventional loans require a 20 percent down payment, but there are some loans where the buyer puts down zero. Remember the amount of your down payment influences your monthly payment and the amount of the interest you will pay. If you choose to do so, you can pay money upfront (called points) to lower your interest rate. However, your best source of in-depth information is always your mortgage specialist.

What is the debt-to-income ratio?

This is sometimes referred to as the loan to ratio value, but simply put, it is your debt ratio (the total of all your obligations) compared to your income. The tried and true rates of 28/36 still apply. While there is some variation, these ratios work and you can feel safe about applying them when you are calculating how much house you can afford to buy.

Do I need an escrow account?

Whether you need it or not, if you have a mortgage, you will have an escrow account. A part of each monthly mortgage payment is set aside in a special account called an escrow account to be used to pay your taxes, insurance and so forth.

What is a good faith estimate?

This is an approximation by your lender of all of the costs included in the closing of your real estate transaction.

What happens after my purchase offer is accepted and I apply for my mortgage?

You work with your mortgage professional to provide all the documentation he or she needs to expedite the financing for your home.

What happens at the final walk through?

You look for any obvious discrepancies in the property. For instance, is everything in the same physical condition as when you last viewed the house? In addition, you will be verifying whether all contractually agreed upon improvements or repairs were made.

What can I use to pay the down payment?

Cash or any available funds. Some, but not all, lenders allow monetary gifts to be used for the down payment. Your best choice is to discuss all the available options with your lender to make sure you comply with all regulations and guidelines.

What is private mortgage insurance (PMI)?

Private mortgage insurance insures the mortgage lender in case of loan default. Mortgage insurance refers to a term insurance policy on the borrower with proceeds to be paid to the beneficiary upon the death of the insured.

If you get a mortgage, your lender will require you to buy private mortgage insurance. The two types of insurance you as the homebuyer are required to buy as protection for the lender are private mortgage insurance and homeowner's insurance.

What does the term APR mean?

In plain English, this is simply the annual percentage rate charged by the lender for a full year of financing.

What is the difference between an adjustable rate mortgage and a mortgage with a fixed rate?

At the outset, an adjustable rate mortgage has a lower interest rate, but the rate is subject to adjustment according to the terms of the contract. For instance, the adjustment might be as often as every year, or every two years and so forth. Adjustable mortgage rates are sometimes tied to the prime interest rate.

In a fixed rate loan, the amount of interest paid is the same throughout the life of the contract. Understanding the different types of home loans (see Chapter 4 for more details) available in the market today helps you make the best decision for your personal situation.

What is an interest rate?

In non-technical language, this is the price paid for borrowing the money from the lender. Interest is what you pay; the interest rate is the amount you will pay.

What are points?

Points are the amount of money you pay upfront to buy down the interest rate for either a temporary or a fixed period.

What is a loan origination fee?

This is a fee charged by the mortgage company to cover their administrative costs. It is typically equivalent to one percent of the loan amount so on a $100,000 mortgage, the origination fee would be $1,000.

What is a lock-in?

You are locking in the interest rate for a certain amount of days, months or weeks.

10 – CLOSE THE SALE AND MOVE!

The loan closing is (almost) the final step in the home buying process. Your real estate agent may refer to this as the closing or the settlement; the terms are synonymous.

Either a settlement agent or the closing attorney, depending on how the lender and seller have agreed to finalize the sales transaction, facilitates the closing. The other attendees are the seller and his or her agent and you and your agent. Closing is an important part of the home buying process because that is when legal titles and all legal rights to the property pass from the seller to you.

While the actual closing process varies from state to state and even from closing agent to closing agent, you can expect to:

1. Sign all the documentation to finalize the home sale.

2. Receive evidence of an executed deed and any other pertinent documentation. The actual deed is mailed to you after it is duly recorded.

3. Pay your closing costs.

Some of the documentation that must be presented at closing includes but is not limited to the following:

1. Appraisal

2. Title Insurance Policy

3. Truth in Lending Statement

4. Termite Inspection Certificate

5. Water and Sewage Certification

6. Mortgage Note

7. Deed of Trust

8. Hazard Insurance Policy

9. Homeowner Insurance Policy (bring proof of payment)

10. Flood Insurance Policy (where applicable)

11. Certificate of Occupancy (CO)

12. Settlement Statement (HUD-1 form)

13. Right of Rescission Disclosure

14. Other documentation as required by law

Prior to closing, you provided all of your required documentation to the lender as part of the loan application process.

Before we go into the next discussion, we want to mention that this is when the true real estate professional is worth his weight in importance and earns his or her commission.

In the days prior to closing, agents must be extremely proactive. This means that, to the extent of their abilities, they ensure everyone involved in the closing is doing what they are supposed to do when they are supposed to be doing it.

Chuck says: As an agent, I cannot count the number of times I have gone to closing only to discover that some attorney, real estate agent, mortgage lender, secretary or someone else neglected to do their job in a timely fashion. You have to be a "bird dog" and nudge everyone involved in the closing process to do what they need to do.

This is where the high tech world lulls some professionals into a false sense of security. They think they can get any task done at the last minute via fax or email, but these electronic marvels are subject to glitches and malfunctions just like any other tool or resource. To help your agent execute a smooth closing, make sure you complete these tasks:

- **Schedule** and perform a final walkthrough of the property. This is your last opportunity to ensure all discrepancies and agreed-upon repairs are mitigated.
- **Confirm** the date, time and location of the closing.
- **Obtain** a certified check for your down payment and closing costs.

Your real estate professional can give you an exact amount prior to closing so you can get your check in plenty of time.

Who Pays What

On the settlement statement, there is a section detailing the closing costs paid by the seller and those paid by the buyer. As a rule of thumb, the seller pays for costs such as making a new deed, the certificate of sewage and potable water, and any other costs that were agreed upon in the sales contracts. The buyer pay points, attorney's fees, documentation and recording fees, postage and so forth.

However, oftentimes the seller agrees to pay additional closing costs such as the points in order to expedite the sale or make the offer more attractive to the buyer. Sometimes closing costs are rolled into the mortgage itself. The bottom line is every contract is different; your agent will answer any questions you may have.

Avoiding Glitches

The odds are your closing will go smoothly without a single hitch. That's because you did your due diligence before you ever started the home buying process, and you surrounded yourself with top-notch professionals to help you through the procedure.

However, there are no guarantees in life, and an ounce of preparation is worth a pound of cure and goes a long way toward avoiding any last-minute delays. Here are three key areas to consider:

1. **Compare your settlement statement to the Good Faith Estimate**.

Make sure you understand both documents completely. If the amount of funds you will need to close the transaction is significantly different, make sure you understand why. Bring a certified check for the exact amount, made out as directed by your loan officer or real estate agent.

2. **Bring all the necessary documentation to closing**.

It is much better to have something and not need it, than to need it and not have it, so feel free to go a little overboard when you are planning what to take to closing. As a minimum, you want to have proof of payment for your homeowner's insurance, your driver's license or a valid photo ID, and your checkbook in case there are any unforeseen charges.

3. **Be ready to move.**

You already confirmed the property was in move-in condition at the final walk through. The sellers should have vacated the property and removed all personal items. This is especially important if tenants rather than the property owner occupied the property.

Once all the paperwork is signed and monies are exchanged, you'll be given the keys and the appropriate documentation for your new home. Congratulations! You succeeded in your journey to become a homeowner, and you can move into your new home and start experiencing the pride of home ownership.

Moving Day

We are almost at the end of our journey together through the home buying process, and we hope you enjoyed the trip as much as we did. While it hasn't always been easy, and you have had to do lots of homework during the procedure, you are now the proud owner of a home that fits your lifestyle, your values, your budget, and most importantly, your dreams.

Before we say our final goodbyes, we want to leave you with some hints, tips and tricks to make moving day more pleasant and less stressful for everyone.

Making a move is usually a four-part process: **planning, packing, moving, and unpacking**. Let's look at each to see how we can streamline the procedure.

Planning

Interior Decorating and Remodeling

During your planning phase, think about any remodeling or repairs you want to make to the property before you move in. For instance, if you want to repaint the interior, replace carpet, or refinish hardwood floors, the process is easier and quicker if you complete these projects before occupying the property. Obviously, laying new carpet is much easier if the workers do not have to move furniture and so forth.

You may want to measure windows and make some decisions about window treatments or other accessories you will need to buy. While you may want to wait until after you move in to purchase these items because there is no sense packing any more items than you have to, it saves you the anxiety of making those choices when you are already stressed out from unpacking and organizing your new home.

Go ahead and have new locks made for the doors, and make any necessary electrical upgrades. For example, if you are planning to add ceiling fans or additional lighting such as track lights, complete those upgrades before the move if possible.

Delegate

Make a list of everyone who will help you move, and notify them of your move-in date. Two or three days before the move, call and reconfirm your helpers. If you are using a professional moving company rather than relying on "friend power," it is still a good idea to reconfirm your appointment and all the pertinent details.

Appoint a moving supervisor if you don't plan to take that role for yourself. Much like a wedding planner is the key person who keeps moving the events of the wedding forward and makes sure everyone is where they are supposed to be at the appointed times, your supervisor works from a master list and makes sure nothing gets left behind or undone.

Document and Protect

Now that you are a homeowner, there are tax deductions from which you benefit. Consult your income tax preparer or the IRS website to see what, if any, deductions you can take for expenses related to your move. This way, you will know which receipts to save and how to document expenses properly.

Create a file for important documents such as insurance policies, birth certificates, immunization records, medical and dental records, prescriptions and so on. Include an up-to-date list of important phone numbers: your doctor, dentist, therapist, lawyer, real estate agent, etc.

If your move includes pets, you need copies of their immunizations and rabies certificate(s) as well. Make sure all pets are wearing identification tags, and keep them in their crates or carriers.

Keep this file with you and hand carry it to your new home rather than taking a chance on packing it and then not being able to locate it quickly in an emergency.

In addition to your documents, keep all necessary prescription medicines and valuables on your person rather than entrusting them to the movers.

Use It Up, Sell It or Give It Away

Have a yard sale and sell the unused, unwanted items you do not plan to move to your new home. Stash the cash away and use it to treat yourself to a nice dinner on moving day when you are tired and hungry.

Use up perishable items and chemicals or other hazardous items that you cannot or do not want to move. Pack items that you use only rarely so you have a jump-start on packing day.

Special Needs

Arrange for child and pet care on moving day. Moving is a traumatic event for little ones and pets, so do your best to keep their stress levels low.

Notify the school system and utility companies about the impeding move. Arrange for school records to be transferred if necessary, and leave forwarding addresses with the utilities if you anticipate receiving any refunds on utility or housing deposits.

Packing

Have plenty of packing supplies on hand such as boxes, wrapping materials (think packing peanuts or bubble wrap), permanent marking pens, tape measure, packing tape, scissors, and old newspapers.

If you kept the original packaging materials from the purchase of large items such as televisions or computers, your safest bet is to repack them in those. If not, put all wiring, cables, screws and other fixtures in a sealable plastic bag and tape the bag to either the item or the box in which it is packed.

If boxes weigh approximately 40 to 50 pounds each, they are easier to stack, load and remove on location. On that note, remember that books are heavy so avoid overloading boxes with too many or they may burst when they are picked up.

Mark each box with the contents, its approximate location on the moving van or truck, and the room it will go to at the new location.

Pack up room-by-room and layer items in boxes: lighter items on top, heavier ones on bottom. Tape the box, label, stack and move on to the next one.

Moving

Let's talk briefly about what you will not be able to move. If you are using a professional moving service, they probably gave you a checklist of their guidelines for items they are not permitted to move. However, if you are making the move yourself, there are some items, which cannot be transported across state lines.

Food, Pets and Plants Can Be Problematic

Check with the U.S. Department of Agriculture or your country extension office before you move food and plants across state lines. Rules and regulations vary widely from state to state, and you want to make sure you comply with the letter of the law.

Houseplants, pets and perishable foods are some of the trickiest items to transport safely. In our experience, if it does not cause you incredible trauma, it's better to give the houseplants away rather than to move them.

If you can't consume all the opened foodstuffs or frozen items before the big day, give unopened, unused foods to friends and neighbors. You'll be amazed at how much relief from moving day stress you will enjoy by letting go of those items and moving on.

Moving Your Pets Safely

The best scenario for pets is to board or place them with a friend for a day or two if possible to keep their stress levels down.

If that is not possible, move them in their crates to give them a sense of being in a somewhat familiar situation, and get them moved into the new house first. For safety reasons, you may want to leave them in their crate or carrier as long as the movers or strangers are present in your new home.

Regulations on pets vary widely from state to state so check ahead to see if your pet needs any health documentation from your veterinarian or if it will have to be quarantined for any length of time.

Unpacking

Do yourself a favor before you start unpacking the first box. Assess your situation and decide which items you need first and where you need to focus your efforts for the maximum result. Wanting to get all the boxes unpacked, the debris hauled away, and everything neatly in its place is a normal response to the chaos of moving, but trying to accomplish it on the same day you move in is not realistic.

Give yourself permission to unpack over the space of a few days, and stop when you start to feel frustrated or fatigued.

As a rule, take care of necessities first, which means you will probably start in the bathroom or kitchen areas first. If you have to leave the mattresses on the floor and have a huge family sleep-in, who cares? You are now the owner of this castle and you can do as you please.

ABOUT THE AUTHORS

Charles "Check with Chuck" Cosmato lives in the Smith Mountain Lake area of Moneta, Virginia with his wife of 66 years, Lillian. Although he is still a licensed associate broker, he's semi-retired from a 26 year career in real estate, which in his opinion means he occasionally, as he says, "comes out of retirement" to work with a select clientele. He has one son and a daughter-in-law, a grandson and granddaughter-in-law, and three great-grandchildren. In addition to his beloved wife, they are the loves of his life.

In addition to being a former licensed real estate agent, Donna Cosmato is an investigative reporter with an established reputation for providing her readers with extensively researched, factual information on a wide variety of topics. Her specialty niche is interviewing experts, and she offers her readers unique answers and advice on their frequently asked questions about pet health, personal finance, real estate, education, autism and other subjects.